The Call

Olayinka Olusola Akisanya

Dedication

This book is dedicated to God Almighty for His faithfulness. So great is Your mercy toward us!

Acknowledgment

Many thanks to my parents and siblings for the love, care, and support they have shown me.

To you, Demilade, words alone cannot express my profound gratitude for your love, support, and encouragement toward the completion of this book.

To my priceless jewel, Oluwadarasimi, thank you for your undying love through thick and thin.

About the Author

Olayinka Akisanya is a devoted child of God who has a message of God's Relentless Acts of Compassion and Empowerment (GRACE) for this and every generation. Her books, like her life, encapsulates and lays bare before readers the amazing strength we can draw from the word of God in dire straits of life's journey. She is also the author of *"Surviving the Opposite,"* which is her first published book.

Olayinka is a humble, multi-talented woman of God who lives in the United States of America.

Preface

This book is not only for those people who are having trouble with their faith. It is about the conviction, perseverance, and patience that one needs to have because there is a purpose. I wish everyone gets to know that we all came to this earth with a purpose from God. That purpose can only be revealed to all of us if we persevere through all the phases of life; good and bad.

The troubles in life can have people questioning their faith. This book will help you find hope and strength to persevere through all your tests and trials in life so you can become the stout, loyal follower of God that you were always meant to be. We all have the strength in us; we just need to find it. And this book is what will help you discover your inner strengths and utilize them to win all the rewards that He promised us.

Contents

Page Left Blank Intentionally

Introduction

We all go through different phases of life. Either good or bad, they are all part of our destiny. A destiny curated by God. When we suffer and go through troubling times, it is because God has chosen us for his trials. When God selects an individual, it is because that person has a specific mission to fulfill. The truth is that many receive the call, but only a few people are chosen. This can be elaborated by what Jesus said:

"14 For many are called, but few are chosen." **Matthew 22:14 (KJV)**

Everyone who holds steadfast to their faith has been called, but the call is based on obedience. On the other hand, the ones who were chosen by God were predestined for their fate. Their trials and tests of faith were predetermined by God so that they could truly prove their loyalty and obedience.

"29 For those God foreknew he also predestined to be conformed to the image of his Son, that he might be the firstborn among many brothers and sisters. 30 And those he

predestined, he also called; those he called, he also justified; those he justified, he also glorified." **Romans 8:29 – 30 (NIV)**

All of those who are chosen receive the call, but not all who receive the call are the chosen ones. Those who have faith and receive the call, as well as those who are chosen, go through a set of trials and tribulations in life. It is the nature, strength, duration, and purpose of those trials faced that really marks the difference between those who are called from those who were chosen.

"12 In fact, everyone who wants to live a godly life in Christ Jesus will be persecuted." **2 Timothy 3:12 (NIV)**

Throughout the Bible, from the Old Testament to the New, many of those that were chosen by God faced trials that reflected what their mission was about. Many great examples in the Bible reflect how such tests are meant for everyone so that they could prove their obedience. Noah was chosen, and his trial was about saving god-fearing people from destruction. He had to build an ark and collect all the required animals before the flood could start wreaking havoc. Moses was another follower that God chose. His Godly mission was to deliver the Israelites that were suffering at the hands of the Pharaoh. His trials began all the way since his birth and continued throughout his life. He suffered through hardships that were destined for him by God up until his mission was fulfilled. His task was monumental, and so were his trials.

As described in the New Testament, Jesus Christ was also one of the chosen ones. He was granted the purpose of redeeming the people of the world. He was meant to bring the astray back to God. So, all his trials reflected His mission. Peter was another chosen one, but he was definitely not the last. The list goes on and on. If we wish to be used by God, we must first be firm believers and followers. That is done through confessing and believing that Jesus is our Lord and was raised from death by God.

*"9 If you declare with your mouth, "Jesus is Lord," and believe in your heart that God raised him from the dead, you will be saved." **Romans 10: 9 (NIV)***

The next step is to be willing and obedient to God's words and instructions. This book is designed to help believers know what it takes to be called and chosen (used) by God.

Chapter 1
The Purpose of Trial

"12 From the days of John the Baptist until now, the kingdom of heaven has been subjected to violence, and violent people have been raiding it."

-Matthew 11:12 (NIV)

As the scripture explains, every single creature of God goes through trials and tribulations. Heaven and Earth are filled with creatures that follow the word of God. These creatures are all bound by destiny to go through violent tribulations. They are all meant to suffer the tests of God, which could include violent circumstances. History is full of events that prove how God's most obedient and loyal followers had to go through many battles and hard times. Their trials were predestined for them, and their faith was their only weapon.

"20 For the creation was subjected to frustration, not by its own choice, but by the will of the one who subjected it, in hope 21 that[a] the creation itself will be liberated from its

*bondage to decay and brought into the freedom and glory of the children of God." **Romans 8:20 (NIV)***

There are battles to fight, be it physical or spiritual. Physical battles were fought throughout history by men of God. They fought those battles, no matter how bleak or hopeless their circumstances were. They only had the flame of faith burning deep inside their hearts to keep them going. They used its fire to burn down the hate and ignorance of those that strayed from the path of God. They had to go through hardships that included starving themselves, losing their homes and loved ones, and facing the contempt of the society. They had nothing that gave them an advantage against their enemies.

However, those battles are only tests of faith. They are meant to prepare the chosen ones for the bigger battle that is yet to come. The war that is associated with fulfilling one's true purpose in life here on Earth. In other words, God wants to show us who He is so we can discover who we truly are. Since the beginning of time, we have gotten many examples of the chosen ones and those that were called by God. They went through trials of their own to learn and know who God really **is**. Those people include:

- Abraham, Olayinka Akisanya (Author) - God is a Provider and Covenant keeping God.

- Moses, Author - God is a Deliverer and Way-maker.

- Joshua, Author- God, is a Mighty Warrior.

- Ezekiel, Job, Author- God is a Restorer (Giver of life).

- Daniel, Author- God is a Protector.

- Hezekiah, Job, Kenneth Haggins, Bishop Oyedepo, Author- God is a Healer.

- Hebrew boys, Author- God is a Protector and Comforter.

- Peter, Author- God is a Solid Rock and Miracle worker.

- Paul, Author- God is a Rescuer and Savior.

- Jacob, Author- God is a Patient God.

- Joseph, Author- God is a Forgiving God.

- Bishop T.D Jakes, Author- God is a Rewarder of those who diligently seek Him.

- Kenneth Haggins, Bishop Oyedepo, Pastor E.A Adeboye, Author- God is a Faith-full and Faithful God.

- Jesus Christ and All- God is the only Savior, Giver of Life, the Only Way, the Immortal, Invisible God, and the King of all Kings.

This is similar to a setting where the people in authority train their chosen fighters for upcoming battles. For instance, any government in a country selects the most capable people among its citizens as soldiers. Then they train these chosen soldiers to train and learn how to fight for the country and its people in advance for future battles. It includes all kinds of training, tests, and practices to prepare the soldiers for the hard battle that is yet to come.

They use all their resources and skills to get ready to defend their homeland and its inhabitants. And if the likelihood of war climbs more and more every day, the intensity of the training doubles. The more that they are in danger of being at war, the harder they train. And such training continues until the battle day arrives. And during the training, there can be some that buckle under pressure, or are not as committed to the cause. They are deemed unfit for the upcoming battle because they fell along the way even before the war meant that they were not capable of defending the cause. So when it comes to the kingdom of God, the chosen ones do not get to pick the kind of trials they go through or the battles they fight. More often than not, the chosen ones get to learn what their purpose is. And other times, the chosen one has to inquire of God.

"³ His divine power has given us everything we need for a godly life through our knowledge of him who called us by his own glory and goodness. 4 Through these he has given us his very great and precious promises, so that through them you may participate in the divine nature, having escaped the corruption in the world caused by evil desires." **2 Peter 1:3-4 (NIV)**

God has dealt out a measure of grace for every chosen one. It is so that it could sustain the individuals during their trials. These trials are considered as processes that help build and strengthen faith. In one of Dr. Charles' messages, he identifies the purpose of these trials that the chosen ones have to go through as follows:

- A cleaning and purification process

- A test of faith by getting us to:

- Push the limit

- Build saints and conform us to Christ

- Prove our devotion to our Lord Jesus Christ; *"10 The death he died, he died to sin once for all; but the life he lives, he lives to God."* **Romans 6:10 (NIV)**

- Prove our love for Christ

- Prove our steadfastness

- God wants to demonstrate His power to sustain us. *"29 For those God foreknew he also predestined to be conformed to the image of his Son, that he might be the firstborn among many brothers and sisters."* **Romans 8:29 (NIV)**

The level of the trials and tribulations that a chosen one has to go through depends on certain things. It depends on the amount of grace God has **given** to the individual to help them overcome their hardships with the strongest faith. It is also based on the fact as to how much pressure is needed to activate the power of God (anointing) in a person's life. With these things, you are able to judge the intensity of your trials.

And once you have figured that out, you could even find a way to discover your purpose in life.

Chapter 2
The Cost of the Oil

"29 You shall consecrate them so they will be most holy, and whatever touches them will be holy."

-(Exodus 30:29)

In the Bible, oil is the symbol of the Holy Spirit. It represents the power and presence of God and the Holy Spirit. 'Anointing' someone means to pour over or smear onto them. Anointing by oil is a representation of the Holy Spirit being poured over God's child. It sanctifies a person and sets them apart as holy. The anointing oil is a symbol of the power of God.

When God created Man, He embedded His power in him. **God is aware of this power, the devil fears it, but man is not aware of it. God** empowered us to make decisions. **This** is the greatest ability and power God gave Man. When a person accepts Jesus Christ in their heart and acknowledges Him as Lord and Savior, the Holy Spirit helps them recognize how God's power is present in their lives. They become aware of the power God imbedded in them upon creation. Once the person has become aware of God's power present in them, the next step is to activate it. The only way to activate that power in us is to go through trials.

So, God **allows** trials **to come** our way, which will help strengthen our faith **and** also activate His power in us. Our Savior, Jesus Christ, prepared us for such trials ahead of time:

"I have told you these things so that in me you may have peace. In this world, you will have trouble. But take heart! I have overcome the world." (John 16:33)

Jesus, fully man and God, knew that when He returns to the Father, the devil will contend with the power that we hold within us. Initially, when God created the world and us, he did not intend for us to suffer. He did not want us to go through trials when He created us in His image. But then the devil realized that man had not yet become aware of the power of God in him, **that was** when he decided to trick Eve. He hoodwinked her into going against the word of God and sin**ned** with Adam. They sold the power they held to the devil. That is how man lost their power, and the devil was able to hold so much power over the world.

Since the earth became the devil's territory, he constantly set up roadblocks and distractions for humans in the form of trials, tragedies, death, sickness, etc. He wanted to prevent human beings from becoming aware of the power Jesus Christ came to restore unto Man.

"The thief comes only to steal and kill and destroy; I have come that they may have life and have it to the full." (John 10:10)

God knows how clever the devil is. He knew that he would be after the restored power in man so, God hid the Restored Power in Jesus Christ. He gave us the power through His Holy Spirit.

"Here is my servant whom I have chosen, the one I love, in whom I delight;

I will put my Spirit on him, and he will proclaim justice to the nations." (Matthew 12:18)

Apart from having eternal life and making it to the kingdom of God, the power that we gain through the Holy Spirit of God is another reason why Man must accept Jesus Christ as his Lord and Savior – why he should worship and serve Him only.

"As for me, this is my covenant with them," says the Lord. "My Spirit, who is on you, will not depart from you, and my words that I have put in your mouth will always be on your lips, on the lips of your children and on the lips of their descendants—from this time on and forever," says the Lord."
(Isaiah 59:21)

The moment an individual becomes aware of the Restored Power by accepting Jesus Christ as Lord and Savior, the devil tries his hardest to delay or prevent **the person** from activating that power. He starts by providing distractions from peers and family in the form of opposition, ridicule, and negativity toward one's faith and belief in Jesus Christ.

"Everyone will hate you because of me, but the one who stands firm to the end will be saved." ***(Mark 13:13)***

If the devil is unable to break a man at that point, he moves on to the pre-trial phase. This consists of various kinds of trials ranging from hatred to loss, sickness, depression, death, and the list goes on (Matt 11:12). Many people buckle during the distraction phase and never get to go through the trial phase. The devil then rewards those who fall by giving them an alternative reward (sin), so he could

14

pull the **people** away from returning to faith even more. Some of these rewards could include a lack of remorse, disobedience, bitterness, anger, depression, love for money, lust, isolation, insecurity, **unforgiveness,** and more.

*"Be alert and of sober mind. Your enemy, the devil, prowls around like a roaring lion looking for someone to devour. 9 Resist him, standing firm in the faith, because you know that the family of believers throughout the world is undergoing the same kind of sufferings." **(1 Peter 5:8-9)***

The devil gives such fruits in exchange for the Fruits of the Spirit.

*"But the fruit of the Spirit is love, joy, peace, forbearance, kindness, goodness, faithfulness" **(Galatians 5:22)***

*"The fruit of the righteous is a tree of life; and he that winneth souls is wise." **Prov 11: 30 (KJV)***

It is important to get rid of the devil's rewards to be able to progress forward into the trial phase.

*"Get rid of all bitterness, rage, and anger, brawling and slander, along with every form of malice." **(Ephesians 4:31)***

"Therefore, get rid of all moral filth and the evil that is so

prevalent and humbly accept the word planted in you, which can save you." (James 1:21)

After the distraction (pre-trial phase), the next step is the trial phase. The trials a believer faces depends on the level of their anointing or the power of God that was deposited in them upon creation. In other words, the activation of the Restored Power is directly proportional to the trial an individual faces. Because God deposited His power in man when He created him, and His power can perform all miracles, trials remain constant in a believer's life.

No wonder God instructed us to always pray;

"17 pray continually" (1 Thessalonians 5:17)

"14 Guard the good deposit that was entrusted to you— guard it with the help of the Holy Spirit who lives in us." (2 Timothy 1:14)

Our trials are designed just like battles. We have to fight the distractions as well as the urge to give up. Apart from the activation of the Restored Power, trials also strengthen a believer's faith remarkably. Apostle Paul prepares us in advance for the Christian walk:

"Fight the good fight of the faith. Take hold of the eternal life to which you were called when you made your good confession in the presence of many witnesses." **(1 Timothy 6:12)**

While the devil uses trials and distractions to trip believers off the Christian walk, God allows it all to strengthen a believer's faith. As the whole point of being a Christian and a believer is to please God, we must build up our faith.

"And without faith, it is impossible to please God, because anyone who comes to him must believe that he exists and that he rewards those who earnestly seek him." **(Hebrews 11:6)**

"20 But you, dear friends, by building yourselves up in your most holy faith and praying in the Holy Spirit, 21 keep yourselves in God's love as you wait for the mercy of our Lord Jesus Christ to bring you to eternal life." **(Jude 1:20-21)**

"19 holding on to faith and a good conscience, which some have rejected and so have suffered shipwreck with regard to the faith." **(1 Timothy 1:19)**

God's love for His children is so intense that He longs to see His children use the power He deposited in them. He wants them to do greater works than Jesus did while He was on earth.

"12 Very truly I tell you, whoever believes in me will do the works I have been doing, and they will do even greater things than these because I am going to the Father." (John 14:12)

But the only way we can activate this power is through trials. While trials are not necessarily always from God, He permits them to be able to activate His power in us. The key factors to persevere through the trial phase as part of one's calling are Faith, Hope, Patience, and Perseverance - Endurance.

"10 You, however, know all about my teaching, my way of life, my purpose, faith, patience, love, endurance," (2 Timothy 3:10)

Chapter 3
Faith

"Now faith is confidence in what we hope for and
assurance about what we do not see."

-(Hebrews 11:1)

According to this verse, faith is about what is in your heart. You believe in something with confidence, even if you cannot see any of it. That is faith; the ability to believe in every word of God without seeing any physical evidence. The cost of the oil is the endurance required to build faith up to the point that it pleases God as Hebrews 11:6 shows. Faith is basically the eyes through which believers are expected to see and walk with God.

That kind of faith comes by hearing the Message and hearing the Message by the Word of God.

"17 Consequently, faith comes from hearing the message,
and the message is heard through the word about Christ."
(Romans 10:17)

Faith is not growing in many believers these days because the message they are hearing is NOT the Word of God. There are too many preachers out there like they have always been since the day of John the Baptist. They preach what their congregations want to hear to satisfy their needs, and increase the number of their congregations. While miracles are experienced because every name has to bow to the name of Jesus Christ, faith in God does not grow in the miracle seeking believers. It grows in the actions of the person who is doing miracles in a season. The **God kind of** faith grows and develops in stages through trials. The source of that faith **is** in God's Word, and there are levels to it (Faith).

"12 In fact, everyone who wants to live a godly life in Christ Jesus will be persecuted, 13 while evildoers and impostors will go from bad to worse, deceiving and being deceived. 14 But as for you, continue in what you have learned and have become convinced of, because you know those from whom you learned it, 15 and how from infancy you have known the Holy Scriptures, which are able to make you wise for salvation through faith in Christ Jesus. 16 All Scripture is God-breathed and is useful for teaching, rebuking, correcting, and training in righteousness, 17 so

that the servant of God[a] may be thoroughly equipped for every good work." (2 Timothy 3:12-17)

There is only one Biblical definition of Faith in **Hebrews 11:1**, but, there are many types of Faith. The Biblical description of the kinds of Faith include:

- **No Faith**

"40 He said to his disciples, "Why are you so afraid? Do you still have no faith?" (Mark 4:40)

- **Little Faith** *(NIV) Unbelief (KJV) Your Lack of Trust and Confidence in the Power of God (AMP) Not yet taking God Seriously (MSG) Don't Have Enough (NLT),*

"20 He replied, "Because you have so little faith. Truly I tell you, if you have faith as small as a mustard seed, you can say to this mountain, 'Move from here to there,' and it will move. Nothing will be impossible for you." (Matthew 17:20)

- **Weak Faith**

"2 One person's faith allows them to eat anything, but another, whose faith is weak, eats only vegetables." (Romans 14:2)

"2 And so it was with me, brothers and sisters. When I came to you, I did not come with eloquence or human wisdom as I proclaimed to you the testimony about God.[a] 2 For I resolved to know nothing while I was with you except Jesus Christ and him crucified. 3 I came to you in weakness with great fear and trembling." **(1 Corinthians 2:3)**

• Strong or Firm Standing Faith

"13 Be on your guard; stand firm in the faith; be courageous; be strong." **(1 Corinthians 16:13)**

"Timothy Joins Paul and Silas

16 Paul came to Derbe and then to Lystra, where a disciple named Timothy lived, whose mother was Jewish and a believer but whose father was a Greek. 2 The believers at Lystra and Iconium spoke well of him. 3 Paul wanted to take him along on the journey, so he circumcised him because of the Jews who lived in that area, for they all knew that his father was a Greek. 4 As they traveled from town to town, they delivered the decisions reached by the apostles and elders in Jerusalem for the people to obey. 5 So the churches were strengthened in the faith and grew daily in numbers." **(Acts:16)**

*"11 I long to see you so that I may impart to you some spiritual gift to make you strong," (**Romans 1:11**)*

*"24 Not that we lord it over your faith, but we work with you for your joy, because it is by faith you stand firm." (**2 Corinthians 1:24**)*

1 Tim 1:19,

*"14 What good is it, my brothers and sisters if someone claims to have faith but has no deeds? Can such faith save them?" (**James 2:14**)*

"Be strong and take heart,

all you who hope in the Lord." (Psalm 31:24)

- **Great Faith**

*"10 When Jesus heard this, he was amazed and said to those following him, "Truly I tell you, I have not found anyone in Israel with such great faith." (**Matthew 8:10**)*

*"28 Then Jesus said to her, "Woman, you have great faith! Your request is granted." And her daughter was healed at that moment." (**Matthew 15:28**)*

"9 When Jesus heard this, he was amazed at him and turning to the crowd following him, he said, "I tell you, I

have not found such great faith even in Israel." (Luke 7:9) Many pastors have different descriptions of the types of faith there are. For instance, there is a series of messages called **"CRAZY FAITH"** by Pastor Michael Todd of Transformation Church (TC) in Tulsa, Oklahoma. Pastor Todd described some of the types of faith or the levels of faith as *Crazy Faith, Baby Faith, Maybe Faith, Wavy Faith, Daily Faith* (Pastor Brie Davis, TC), *Hazy Faith* (Pastor Jeremy Foster - Houston), *Lazy Faith, Trading Faith, Hasty Faith, and Hasty Faith (FOMO).* I strongly recommend everyone to listen to their messages and more on their YouTube channel.

God began to unfold the revelation of the types of faith to me one evening while I was driving home from the treatment center. I got the revelation that the types of Faith can be seen as driving a manual transmission vehicle (Stick-Shift). To all who are able to drive a stick-shift vehicle, I want you to recall your first exposure and experience with driving a stick-shift. Most probably, if you learned how to drive a stick-shift vehicle as a young adult (18 - 20 years), it was because that was all that was available or presented to you by your parents or peers. It was probably not by choice.

Crazy Faith is the willingness to accept what is presented to you for the first time with the intention to complete the task (BELIEVE) without hesitation. *Crazy Faith* takes charge of a situation at the moment automatically. *Crazy Faith* generally takes off your abilities and trust in yourself and places it in someone greater (more qualified, experienced, or masterful); God. *Crazy Faith* says: *Yes, Lord! Yes, to your will!*

Baby Faith, on the other hand, is the first step taken in obedience towards accomplishing the task. With the stick-shift analogy, holding the car keys and sitting at the driver's seat is the *Baby Faith*.

Baby Faith agrees with *Crazy Faith* enough to launch the first move without any experience or guarantee that it will work out well. Filled with doubt of failure and possibility of success, the learner inserts the key into the ignition and most often starts the vehicle without waiting for the command to begin, simply because that's the next step, and it appears easy.

Some trainers may let you start the vehicle without giving the instruction to ' push down the crutch while starting the vehicle.' Just because the learner gave the impression that

he/she can start the vehicle by not asking, other trainers may decide to give the instructions anyways (inquired by a learner or not). The goal of the trainer is to never discourage the learner but to (1) know how much the learner knows about stick-shift, and (2) that the learner could experience what happens when things are not done the right way.

God, on the other hand, may not prevent a fall or incident when someone launches without getting instructions or permission to carry out a God-ordained task. Not that He does not already know, but that He is checking one's level of knowledge and faith in Him. As well as for the individual to experience what happens when you disobey.

Now that the engine is running, *Maybe Faith* shifts the gear into the first gear, thinking that the car will launch forward and begin to move upon releasing the clutch and gas pedals. If both pedals are released too soon, the car does launch forward in a jerky motion, stalls, and the engine is cut off. This is the hardest part to learn and master when driving a stick-shift. As regards to *Maybe Faith*, this kind of faith launches toward an obstacle with a mindset - maybe it will work or it won't (Doubt- double minded).

"8 A double minded man is unstable in all his ways."
(James 1:8)

This explains why the first launch into God's purpose for one's life is challenging and comes with a stumble. The stumble is not a bad thing at this point, so long as the Maybe faith is used positively. This means 'maybe I'll make it the second time.' ***Maybe Faith*** thrives on Hope. The flip side of Hope at this stage is discouragement and frustration. The battle that must be fought at the ***Maybe Faith*** level is the urge to quit or give up on God. The next level of faith includes ***Wavy Faith, Daily Faith, and Hazy Faith***.

With a ***Wavy, Daily, and Hazy Faith***, the learner continues to drive smoothly along the same straight path or road until there is a turn to make. The turn in this analogy represents a change in plan or an unforeseen obstacle such as sickness, loss, death, or tragedy of any other kind. Navigating through this period is very challenging because it takes the learner to first, be aware of an upcoming turn so as to begin to downshift the gear to reduce the car's speed and make a safe turn. Secondly, to have the gear in the 2nd for a safe turning. While it is extremely painful and difficult when it comes to ***Wavy, Daily, and Hazy Faith***, it is the faith that says: 'No matter what happens, I know God is for me and if He allows this, He will bring me out. I don't know how, but I know who will bring me out'. These types of faiths test **our** belief in God. During this phase, it appears as though God is silent and no longer speaks or that He has abandoned His own. These types of faith give room for questioning God such as *"Why me?"*, *"If you are who you said you are, why did this happen to me?"* **Also, these types of faiths make it easy to slip into** feeling guilty of some sins, facing depression, or (ultimately) giving up faith. Many believers backslide at this level because these kinds of faith are blurry, and one stumbles too many times. These kinds of faith produce a result, depending on how they are viewed; weak (pessimistic) or stubborn (optimistic). If viewed as weak, the individual gives up faith but, if viewed as stubborn, the individual stands.

"The head of Ephraim is Samaria,

and the head of Samaria is only Remaliah's son.

If you do not stand firm in your faith,

you will not stand at all."' **(Isaiah 7:9)**

Now that the learner has safely maneuvered the turn and has driven along a straight road/ path, the learner would think there are no new skills that must be learned. With the type and level of faith, *Lazy Faith* comes in to play. *Lazy Faith* is a complacent faith, filled with many excuses as to why something cannot, should not, or must not be done. *Lazy Faith* does not see the necessity to carry on. Lazy faith, in other words, is NO faith. This is the point where the learner begins to give excuses such as: 'I'm tired, no need to drive any further.'

Believers with *Lazy Faith* give up easily at the slightest obstacle or opposition. This is where many **lose faith**. They focus more on the problems rather than on God. *Lazy Faith* is the most dangerous kind of faith for believers.

According to Apostle Paul in *1 Timothy 1:19*, we all are instructed to hold on to *"faith and a good conscience, which some have rejected and so have suffered shipwreck with regard to the faith."* *Lazy Faith* exposes a believer to self-condemnation, feelings of worthlessness, insecurity, frustration, depression, and guilt. *Lazy Faith* seeks consolation in other things that negates the ultimate **purpose** and will of God for ones' life. *Lazy Faith* leads to destruction. While there are so many other techniques to be learned with driving a stick-shift vehicle, the learner with patience will have to wait for the trainer to introduce the skills at the trainer's time. The trainer's time is based on how well the learner has mastered the previous skills: shifting gears back and forth, balancing both clutch and gas pedals to keep the car running without stalling while in gear at a stop, etc. The learner fights the urge to quit and trades all excuses for the hope of getting better with repeated practice. The learner needs a lot of patience and hope to overcome Lazy faith. To overcome **Lazy Faith**, **Trading Faith** is required.

Trading Faith is the faith that exchanges **Fear** with **Trust in God** and **Excuses** with **Hope**.

"Trust in the Lord with all your heart and lean not on your own understanding;" **(Prov 3:5)**

In other words, **Trading Faith** is the *"Faith of Jesus Christ,"* according to Dr. Dharius Daniels of Change Church in a message: *"I Need It Back."* Dr. Daniels describes *"Faith of Jesus Christ as Courage."* Trading faith is a stubborn faith-filled with tenacity (courage). Trading faith focuses on God and His Word. Trading faith is anchored on the finished works of God (Grace) and His ability to perform miracles.

30

Trading faith sees victory in every situation. *Trading Faith* is generally beaten up by the cares of this world but relentlessly fights against giving up. *Trading Faith* is a classic faith of walking by faith, not by sight. It fulfills the scriptures.

"In the past, God spoke to our ancestors through the prophets at many times and in various ways" *(Hebrews 1:1)*

"7 For we live by faith, not by sight." *(2 Corinthians 5:7)*

In a sense, *Trading Faith* resembles *Wavy, Daily, or Hazy faith* except that *Trading Faith* DOES NOT question God. It has enough courage to believe against all the odds. *Trading Faith* has survived many hardships and trials and is confident that God is working all things out for good. (*"28 And we know that in all things God works for the good of those who love him, who have been called according to his purpose."* *(Romans 8:28)*

"6 being confident of this, that he who began a good work in you will carry it on to completion until the day of Christ Jesus." *(Phillip 1:6)* Patience is the by-product of *Trading Faith* – the patience to wait and keep on fighting until God awards the victory or prize.

"12 Therefore, since we are surrounded by such a great cloud of witnesses, let us throw off everything that hinders and the sin that so easily entangles. And let us run with perseverance the race marked out for us, 2 fixing our eyes on Jesus, the pioneer and perfecter of faith. For the joy set before him, he endured the cross, scorning its shame, and sat down at the right hand of the throne of God. 3 Consider him who endured such opposition from sinners, so that you will not grow weary and lose heart.

God Disciplines His Children

*4 In your struggle against sin, you have not yet resisted to the point of shedding your blood." **(Hebrews 12: 1-4)***

"8 What is more, I consider everything a loss because of the surpassing worth of knowing Christ Jesus my Lord, for whose sake I have lost all things. I consider them garbage, that I may gain Christ 9 and be found in him, not having a righteousness of my own that comes from the law, but that which is through faith in[a] Christ—the righteousness that comes from God on the basis of faith. 10 I want to know Christ—yes, to know the power of his resurrection and participation in his sufferings, becoming like him in his death, 11 and so, somehow, attaining to the resurrection

from the dead.

"12 Not that I have already obtained all this, or have already arrived at my goal, but I press on to take hold of that for which Christ Jesus took hold of me. 13 Brothers and sisters, I do not consider myself yet to have taken hold of it. But one thing I do: Forgetting what is behind and straining toward what is ahead, 14 I press on toward the goal to win the prize for which God has called me heavenward in Christ Jesus." (Philippians 3:8-14)

The flip side of **Trading Faith** is **Hasty Faith**. **Hasty Faith** is fueled by fear. In other words, **Hasty Faith** is a fear-driven faith. It is devoid of patience and tends to act without God's permission. It is equivalent to releasing the clutch too soon while driving a stick-shift vehicle. With the premature act, the vehicle jerks, stalls, and impedes movement.

Hasty Faith makes a bad situation worse. It is stepping out of God's plan for one's life and hoping God blesses the action. God is only committed to fulfilling His purpose, plan, and promise in the life of an obedient follower. Lastly, while **Trading Faith** feeds the vision, plan, and purpose of God for one's life, **Hasty Faith** kills it.

Chapter 4
Hope

During the trial phase, we can face trials that test our faith and its limit. It means that we are on the verge of either strengthening our faith or losing it altogether. That is why we are taught never to lose hope. Hope can be your only weapon to defeat the devil and persevere through the trials. Hope is a key factor in getting past the trial phase successfully with your faith intact and get to one's true calling or purpose.

According to the word of God, hope can be viewed as: fully trusting in God and His word, believing that a difficult situation is possible to turn around for good as all things are possible with God. Hope follows the light of God's word and His ability to do all things. Hope walks hand in hand with Faith. While faith in God speaks of trusting God's ability to do something, *hope* speaks of one's ability to be a recipient of God's promises. In other words, hope is the future expectation of something received by faith.

*"In the past, God spoke to our ancestors through the prophets at many times and in various ways." **(Hebrews 1:1 NIV)***

Apostle Paul makes a clear distinction between what *hope* is and what *hope* is not when he said:

*"For in this hope we were saved. But hope that is seen is no hope at all. Who hopes for what they already have?" **(Romans 8:24)***

This means that *hope* speaks of the future.

Furthermore, hope has many different positive attributes. These attributes are considered as fruits of the Spirit that allow your faith to keep getting stronger. With these attributes, you learn how to spread positivity in the world. These attributes are the symbol of God's loyal follower.

*"But the fruit of the Spirit is love, joy, peace, patience, kindness, goodness, faithfulness" **(Galatians 5:22)***

The attributes of hope help us understand the world and humanity much better. We develop empathy, which is hard to come by. Once you achieve these attributes, especially love and kindness, you can follow God's word with much ease. These qualities help make your transition smooth.

You can beat the trails you face using these attributes. If you face animosity or hatred, you can combat it using love and kindness. If you face violence, you can combat it with peace. If you face hardships, you can combat it with patience. And if you face evil and injustice, you can beat it with the help of faithfulness and goodness of the heart. As long as you have these attributes, you can face anything because they give you the strength to carry on and fight.

Lastly, *hope* rests entirely in God's finished works – Grace.

"8 For it is by grace you have been saved, through faith— and this is not from yourselves, it is the gift of God— 9 not by works so that no one can boast." **(Ephesians 2:8-9)**

What comes to your mind when you think of Grace? Is it the limitless favor shown to us by God? Whenever God does something for us, it is imbued with His Grace. He is gracious in every action he takes or every word He bestows upon us. When He plans our future, blesses us with His mercy and salvation, equips the saints, or convicts the sinners, all of His actions are infused with Grace. He bestows his Grace on His creation because through it all; He loves all.

"The Lord is not slow in keeping his promise, as some understand slowness. Instead, he is patient with you, not wanting anyone to perish, but everyone to come to repentance." **(2 Peter 3:9)**

Patience and perseverance, as stated earlier, are also attributes of hope. They are also known as endurance.

"But if we hope for what we do not yet have, we wait for it patiently." **(Romans 8:25)**

Chapter 5
Patience

"The fear of the Lord is the beginning of knowledge, but fools[a] despise wisdom and instruction."

-Proverbs 1:7 NIV

"It is because of him that you are in Christ Jesus, who has become for us wisdom from God—that is, our righteousness, holiness, and redemption."

-1 Corinthians 1:30

"Make every effort to live in peace with everyone and to be holy; without holiness, no one will see the Lord."

-(Hebrews 12:14)

Wondering what the bible verses have got to do with *patience*? It is because the goal of our faith in Jesus Christ is to be *redeemed*, made holy and *righteous* so that we can see God. Patience is what the loyal followers of the Lord and

Savior are blessed with in abundance. Throughout history, we have evidence of prophets and men of God suffering. They had harsh trials to face and experience. They had the virtue of patience to help them through it all. They dealt with it because they had Jesus in their hearts. All this is possible only with *wisdom,* which is Jesus Christ, as explained in *1 Corinthians 1:30 NIV.* The fear of the Lord is the foundation of knowledge that produces wisdom, as elaborated in *Proverbs 1:7 NIV.* And *wisdom* yields *patience.* True wisdom comes with strong faith.

It is the knowledge that God is the only authority when it comes to anything. Without His providence and grace, we would be nothing. He made us capable of persevering through the hardest of trials and tests. He gave us the wisdom that with his support and love, we can conquer anything. That is wisdom. The knowledge that everything we experience leads to Him and our salvation. With such knowledge, we gain the virtue of patience.

"A person's wisdom yields patience;

*it is to one's glory to overlook an offense." **(Proverbs 19:11)***

Patience, in other words, is to wait for God or His timing. Patience is to put yourself completely at His mercy and hope for salvation. You don't know when you will be blessed with it, but you have the wisdom and knowledge that it will be given nonetheless. And His rewards are always on time. When the time is right for you to be rewarded, you earn them.

God has given us His promise that we will be rewarded for all our trials and show of faith and loyalty.

"No weapon forged against you will prevail,

and you will refute every tongue that accuses you.

This is the heritage of the servants of the Lord,

and this is their vindication from me,"

*declares the Lord." **(Isaiah 54:17 NIV)***

That proves that no matter the tests or trials we go through, the followers of God who remain steadfast in their trial phase not only get to reap the rewards of their patience, but also become superior in this life and the one after from those who are not of faith.

"Let us hold unswervingly to the hope we profess, for he who promised is faithful." (Hebrews 10:23 NIV)

Patience is anchored by perseverance. Through your trial phase, you are judged based on various qualities and virtues. Patience is one of the most important ones. It is another key that, along with hope, can help you win the trial phase and move on to the next. With patience, you can endure any suffering that comes along the way. Devil doesn't have patience, which is why it is the best way to beat him and his evil design. He would never be able to harm you or distract you from your faith if you are patient. God will always hold your hand through all your plans.

"Therefore, as God's chosen people, holy and dearly loved, clothe yourselves with compassion, kindness, humility, gentleness, and patience." (Colossians 3:12 NIV)

Chapter 6
Perseverance

Patience and perseverance are sometimes used interchangeably; only that perseverance outlasts patience. While patience is all about tolerance, perseverance, on the other hand, is determination. Tolerance only comes in limited quantities, and it is quite easy to run out of it. But perseverance is long-lasting because determination is harder to let go of. Tolerance is more like a reaction to other people and things, while determination is something that comes from within.

When dealing with difficult human beings, one is expected to be patient with them. But when it comes to our Lord Jesus Christ, both patience and perseverance are required in heavy amounts.

Perseverance is all about how 'God may not show up when I need Him, but He is always on time, and I will wait for Him no matter how long it takes.' God doesn't wait for anyone or anything. He always doles out salvation and rewards at the perfect time. But it takes determination to wait for it. That determination comes with the absolute certainty that no matter how hard your trails are, you will be rewarded for your patience and loyalty.

"But the one who stands firm to the end will be saved." **(Matthew 24:13 NIV)**

The purpose of perseverance is to build Christ-like character (godliness) in believers. Godliness is something we can all achieve through hard work and determination.

"Perseverance, character; and character, hope." **(Romans 5:4 NIV)**

"And to knowledge, self-control; and to self-control, perseverance; and to perseverance, godliness;" **(2 Peter 1:6 NIV)**

Our trials and tribulations are designed to test our faith and thereby produce perseverance, which helps us win in those trails. Perseverance takes us closer to God. It helps us discover our true purpose and calling in this world.

"Because you know that the testing of your faith produces perseverance." **(James 1:3 NIV)**

"Not only so, but we[a] also glory in our sufferings, because we know that suffering produces perseverance;" **(Romans 5:3 NIV)**

Quitting, or not willing to persevere, robs one **of** God's promise. It impedes one's maturity in Christ and compromises the ability to do greater works related to faith growth. The more you lack the will to persevere, the harder your trials will be to go through. You will find yourself alone through it all because God only helps those who have the determination to make it.

"Let perseverance finish its work so that you may be mature and complete, not lacking anything." **(James 1:4 NIV)**

"I know your deeds, your love and faith, your service and perseverance, and that you are now doing more than you did at first." **(Revelation 2:19)**

You wish to be counted as blessed or regarded as the recipient of God's gifts, which include healing, provision, peace, rest, and long life, among others. But for that, one must be willing to persevere through all their hardships and trials.

"As you know, we count as blessed those who have persevered. You have heard of Job's perseverance and have seen what the Lord finally brought about. The Lord is full of compassion and mercy." **(James 5:11 NIV)**

It means that we have to be willing to obey God and forsake habits or characters (sins) that can draw us away from God. Sins such as lack of forgiveness, covetousness, pride (Ego), lack of faith, disobedience, and hatred have to be forsaken to be able to win your trial phase with perseverance.

"Therefore, since we are surrounded by such a great cloud of witnesses, let us throw off everything that hinders and the sin that so easily entangles. And let us run with perseverance the race marked out for us" **(Hebrews 12:1 NIV)**

Chapter 7
The Call

God's calling on a man's life happens after successfully passing the trial phase. At the post-trial phase, the Chosen ones are filled with hope, faith, patience, and perseverance to the degree that God can entrust a mission into **their** hands. At this stage, God has trained the Chosen to a level that he or she can hear and recognize God's still small voice in the midst of chaos (tribulations). And like David,

"Praise be to the Lord my Rock,

who trains my hands for war,

*my fingers for battle." **(Psalm 144:1 NIV)***

Gradually, God begins to unfold His assignment to the Chosen and empowers them to carry it out. The Chosen will face many other challenges, but then it will be with the experience. The faith of God (courage) is seen and used during this phase, and beyond. This is the phase where one is all about God's business and kingdom advancement. In other words, the Chosen has been there, done that, knows and can testify that there is a living God whose name is I AM

THAT I AM. That is, everything you can ever need.

The post-trial phase is very crucial in the life of the Chosen. The trials and tribulations that come with this phase are slightly different than the other trials. The trials and tribulations of the post-trial phase include fighting against LUST and PRIDE (arrogance).

*"For everything in the world-the lust of the flesh, the lust of the eyes, and the pride of life—comes not from the Father but from the world." **(1 John 2:16)***

Since God is committed to fulfilling His promise to give the overcomer a victor's crown:

*"Do not be afraid of what you are about to suffer. I tell you, the devil will put some of you in prison to test you, and you will suffer persecution for ten days. Be faithful, even to the point of death, and I will give you life as your victor's crown." **(Revelation 2:10 NIV)***

All that pertains to life (prosperity/power, influence, health, and longevity) will also be given to the Chosen. Life (the promise) then becomes the target of the devil. The devil will try a different method to carry out his mission; to kill, steal, and destroy the life God promised the Chosen as described in *John 10:10.*

The devil introduces the lust of the flesh (sexual appetite and immorality), the lust of the eye (covetousness), and the pride of life (arrogance) as a bait in exchange for God's promise. Sadly enough, many Chosen have taken the bait of the devil and lost the promise (life) in the process.

The devil first tested out his bait on our Lord Jesus Christ, and he failed. He waited 30 years to try out his plan.

"As soon as Jesus was baptized, he went up out of the water. At that moment, heaven was opened, and he saw the Spirit of God descending like a dove and alighting on him."
(Matthew 3:16 NIV)

The devil did not tempt Jesus before a voice came from heaven and declared Jesus as His Son, but as soon as the announcement declaring Jesus as God's son (fulfillment of the promise) was made, here comes the tempter. The devil offered Jesus the lust of the flesh (appetite - bread), the pride of life (identity and power – questioning Jesus's identity as the Son of God and God's power to send angels to guard Him from falling). And even the lust of the eye (covetousness – riches) as a bait. The first bait from the devil – the lust of the flesh manifests as appetite for worldly things (fame, wealth, attention, praise, and quest for power) and sexual immorality.

Examples of biblical characters who were Chosen but, took the bait (appetite and sexual immorality) include:

(1) King Saul

He sought praise and power, but, when it was not given to him after Goliath was defeated, he became *"very angry."*

"Saul was very angry; this refrain displeased him greatly. "They have credited David with tens of thousands," he thought, "but me with only thousands. What more can he get but the kingdom?" (1 Samuel 18:8 NIV)

King Saul eventually lost his throne and life.

(2) Samson

He was another biblical character who took the bait of lust of the flesh, which manifested in sexual immorality. Samson, though Chosen, engaged in the act of sexual immorality. The act robbed him of his anointing, integrity, and power. He was humiliated and finally died.

"Samson and Delilah

16 One day Samson went to Gaza, where he saw a prostitute. He went in to spend the night with her. 2 The people of Gaza were told, "Samson is here!" So they surrounded the place and lay in wait for him all night at the city gate. They made no move during the night, saying, "At dawn, we'll kill him."

3 But Samson lay there only until the middle of the night. Then he got up and took hold of the doors of the city gate, together with the two posts, and tore them loose, bar and all. He lifted them to his shoulders and carried them to the top of the hill that faces Hebron.

4 Some time later, he fell in love with a woman in the Valley of Sorek, whose name was Delilah. 5 The rulers of the Philistines went to her and said, "See if you can lure him into showing you the secret of his great strength and how we can overpower him so we may tie him up and subdue him. Each one of us will give you eleven hundred shekels[a] of silver."

6 So Delilah said to Samson, "Tell me the secret of your great strength and how you can be tied up and subdued."

7 Samson answered her, "If anyone ties me with seven fresh bowstrings that have not been dried, I'll become as weak as any other man."

8 Then the rulers of the Philistines brought her seven fresh bowstrings that had not been dried, and she tied him with them. 9 With men hidden in the room, she called to him, "Samson, the Philistines are upon you!" But he snapped the bowstrings as easily as a piece of string snaps when it comes close to a flame. So the secret of his strength was not discovered.

10 Then Delilah said to Samson, "You have made a fool of me; you lied to me. Come now, tell me how you can be tied."

11 He said, "If anyone ties me securely with new ropes that have never been used, I'll become as weak as any other man."

12 So Delilah took new ropes and tied him with them. Then, with men hidden in the room, she called to him, "Samson, the Philistines are upon you!" But he snapped the ropes off his arms as if they were threads.

13 Delilah then said to Samson, "All this time, you have been making a fool of me and lying to me. Tell me how you can be tied."

He replied, "If you weave the seven braids of my head into the fabric on the loom and tighten it with the pin, I'll become as weak as any other man." So while he was sleeping, Delilah took the seven braids of his head, wove them into the fabric 14 and[b] tightened it with the pin.

Again she called to him, "Samson, the Philistines are upon you!" He awoke from his sleep and pulled up the pin and the loom, with the fabric.

15 Then she said to him, "How can you say, 'I love you,' when you won't confide in me? This is the third time you have made a fool of me and haven't told me the secret of your great strength." 16 With such nagging, she prodded him day after day until he was sick to death of it.

17 So he told her everything. "No razor has ever been used on my head," he said, "because I have been a Nazirite dedicated to God from my mother's womb. If my head were shaved, my strength would leave me, and I would become as weak as any other man."

18 When Delilah saw that he had told her everything, she sent word to the rulers of the Philistines, "Come back once more; he has told me everything." So the rulers of the Philistines returned with the silver in their hands. 19 After putting him to sleep on her lap, she called for someone to shave off the seven braids of his hair, and so began to subdue him.[c] And his strength left him.

20 Then she called, "Samson, the Philistines are upon you!"

He awoke from his sleep and thought, "I'll go out as before and shake myself free." But he did not know that the Lord had left him.

21 Then the Philistines seized him, gouged out his eyes, and took him down to Gaza. Binding him with bronze shackles, they set him to grinding grain in the prison. 22 But the hair on his head began to grow again after it had been shaved.

The Death of Samson

23 Now the rulers of the Philistines assembled to offer a great sacrifice to Dagon their God and to celebrate, saying, "Our god has delivered Samson, our enemy, into our hands."

24 When the people saw him, they praised their God, saying,

"Our God has delivered our enemy

into our hands,

the one who laid waste our land

and multiplied our slain."

25 While they were in high spirits, they shouted, "Bring out Samson to entertain us." So they called Samson out of the prison, and he performed for them.

When they stood him among the pillars, 26 Samson said to the servant who held his hand, "Put me where I can feel the pillars that support the temple, so that I may lean against them." 27 Now the temple was crowded with men and women; all the rulers of the Philistines were there, and on the roof were about three thousand men and women watching Samson perform. 28 Then Samson prayed to the

Lord, "Sovereign Lord, remember me. Please, God, strengthen me just once more, and let me with one blow get revenge on the Philistines for my two eyes." 29 Then Samson reached toward the two central pillars on which the temple stood. Bracing himself against them, his right hand on the one and his left hand on the other, 30 Samson said, "Let me die with the Philistines!" Then he pushed with all his might, and down came the temple on the rulers and all the people in it. Thus he killed many more when he died than while he lived.

*31 Then his brothers and his father's whole family went down to get him. They brought him back and buried him between Zorah and Eshtaol in the tomb of Manoah his father. He had led[d] Israel twenty years." **(Judges 16 NIV)***

The lust of the eye is another bait the devil uses to derail the Chosen. The lust of the eye primarily manifests as covetousness and or competition. Covetousness is wanting what someone else has while competition is competing with someone. Either way, the lust of the eye is fueled by a lack of contentment. Lack of contentment is the quest for more only to be better than someone at the expense of what God wants for that person (abilities).

The Israelites and King David were classic biblical characters that took the bait of the lust of the eye.

"5 They said to him, "You are old, and your sons do not follow your ways; now appoint a king to lead[a] us, such as all the other nations have." **(1 Samuel 8:5 NIV)**

"19 But the people refused to listen to Samuel. "No!" they said. "We want a king over us. 20 Then we will be like all the other nations, with a king to lead us and to go out before us and fight our battles." **(1 Samuel 8:19-20 NIV)**

This shows us how the Israelites coveted an earthly king in exchange for the KING of KINGS - God. King David also took the bait of the lust of the eye when he coveted Bathsheba (Uriah's wife). As anointed, gifted, and wealthy as David was, covetousness and lack of contentment led him to murder Uriah, stripped him of his confidence. He got humiliated, had a dysfunctional home, and lost some of his children.

"11 In the spring, at the time when kings go off to war, David sent Joab out with the king's men and the whole Israelite army. They destroyed the Ammonites and besieged Rabbah. But David remained in Jerusalem...." **(for the rest**

refer to 2 Samuel 11-13 NIV)

Because King David was not in denial of his evil acts but was remorseful, and he repented (turned away from the evil acts), he received forgiveness from God. The devil uses distorted perception to keep God's children from repenting. This can be simply put as denial, excuses, or self-righteousness. Without repentance, though, people die both physically and spiritually. Regarding repentance, God promises to forgive our sins and restore our land.

"14 if my people, who are called by my name, will humble themselves and pray and seek my face and turn from their wicked ways, then I will hear from heaven, and I will forgive their sin and will heal their land." **(2 Chronicles 7:14 NIV)**

God also expects corresponding actions to prove one's repentance.

"First to those in Damascus, then to those in Jerusalem and in all Judea, and then to the Gentiles, I preached that they should repent and turn to God and demonstrate their repentance by their deeds." **(Acts 26:20 NIV)**

"Produce fruit in keeping with repentance." **(Matt 3: 8 NIV)**

"This is what the Sovereign Lord, the Holy One of Israel, says:

"In repentance and rest is your salvation,

in quietness and trust is your strength,

but you would have none of it. (Isaiah 30: 15 NIV)

Because of God's mercies and unfailing love, He continues to make the sun shine on both the righteous and the evildoer. Similar to the days of Noah and the flood, both the righteous and the evildoer will keep on living. It seems like the evildoer expects God's instant judgment, but, when the judgment tarries, it is mistaken as NO JUDGMENT. Well, *2 Peter 3:9* is a trustworthy saying. This means that without repentance, destruction is inevitable.

The last bait the devil uses to trap God's children is the pride of life (Arrogance). Arrogance is a deadly attribute that does not only trap someone but also erodes one's tendencies and abilities to enjoy God's blessings. Beneath the pride of life is a sense of entitlement. Entitlement to the best of life, such as accolades, wealth, power, fame, and the list goes on and on. In today's life, the pride of life is called *"ego-tripping."* It is the total opposite of humility.

While many may confuse arrogance with *"being principled,"* the latter is expressed with humility. For example, a principled person is humble and does not have *"false pride."* A prideful person, on the other hand, is generally offensive and overbearing. He or she thinks they are better than others, and they display their pride through words and actions.

"To fear the Lord is to hate evil;

I hate pride and arrogance,

evil behavior, and perverse speech." **(Proverbs 8:13 NIV)**

If God did not spare an angel (Lucifer) but rejected him because of pride, God will also reject any unrepentant prideful person.

"Pride goes before destruction,

a haughty spirit before a fall." **(Proverbs 16:18 NIV)**

"When pride comes, then comes disgrace,

but with humility comes wisdom." **(Proverbs 11:2 NIV)**

Here is a test that can help us know if pride is present in our lives.

"Where there is strife, there is pride,

but wisdom is found in those who take advice." (Proverbs 13:10 NIV)

Biblical examples of those who took the bait include but are not limited to the Pharaoh and Queen Vashti. Before Pharaoh and his armies drowned in the red sea, Pharaoh had many opportunities to surrender to God, but because of *"pride,"* his perception of God was distorted. Pharaoh displayed his pride.

"Pharaoh said, "Who is the Lord, that I should obey him and let Israel go? I do not know the Lord, and I will not let Israel go." (Exodus 5:2 NIV)

His persistent, unrepentant heart led him and his army down the path of destruction, and they were all destroyed. Queen Vashti was another biblical character who took the bait and lost her throne as a queen.

"11 to bring before him Queen Vashti, wearing her royal crown, in order to display her beauty to the people and nobles, for she was lovely to look at. 12 But when the attendants delivered the king's command, Queen Vashti refused to come. Then the king became furious and burned

*with anger." **(Esther 1: 11-12 NIV)***

*"Therefore, if it pleases the king, let him issue a royal decree and let it be written in the laws of Persia and Media, which cannot be repealed, that Vashti is never again to enter the presence of King Xerxes. Also, let the king give her royal position to someone else who is better than she." **(Esther 1:19 NIV)***

So many other biblical characters lost either their position or glory for the enemy's bait.

Chapter 8
Victory

God promises us *"life as our victor's crown,"* as elaborated in **Revelation 2:10**. The life God refers to here is *"eternal life."*

"For God so loved the world that he gave his one and only Son, that whoever believes in him shall not perish but have eternal life." **(John 3:16 NIV)**

To every believer who fights the good fight of faith and overcomes, an everlasting life awaits the person in God's kingdom.

"12 Therefore, since we are surrounded by such a great cloud of witnesses, let us throw off everything that hinders and the sin that so easily entangles. And let us run with perseverance the race marked out for us, 2 fixing our eyes on Jesus, the pioneer and perfecter of faith. For the joy set before him, he endured the cross, scorning its shame, and sat down at the right hand of the throne of God. 3 Consider him who endured such opposition from sinners, so that you will not grow weary and lose heart.

God Disciplines His Children

4 In your struggle against sin, you have not yet resisted to the point of shedding your blood. 5 And have you completely forgotten this word of encouragement that addresses you as a father addresses his son? It says,

"My son, do not make light of the Lord's discipline,

and do not lose heart when he rebukes you,

6 because the Lord disciplines the one he loves,

and he chastens everyone he accepts as his son." [a]

7 Endure hardship as discipline; God is treating you as his children. For what children are not disciplined by their father? 8 If you are not disciplined—and everyone undergoes discipline—then you are not legitimate, not true sons and daughters at all. 9 Moreover, we have all had human fathers who disciplined us, and we respected them for it. How much more should we submit to the Father of spirits and live! 10 They disciplined us for a little while as they thought best; but God disciplines us for our good, in order that we may share in his holiness. 11 No discipline seems pleasant at the time, but painful. Later on, however, it produces a harvest of righteousness and peace for those who have been trained by it.

12 Therefore, strengthen your feeble arms and weak knees. 13 "Make level paths for your feet,"[b] so that the lame may not be disabled, but rather healed.

Warning and Encouragement

14 Make every effort to live in peace with everyone and to be holy; without holiness no one will see the Lord. 15 See to it that no one falls short of the grace of God and that no bitter root grows up to cause trouble and defile many. 16 See that no one is sexually immoral, or is godless like Esau, who for a single meal, sold his inheritance rights as the oldest son. 17 Afterward, as you know, when he wanted to inherit this blessing, he was rejected. Even though he sought the blessing with tears, he could not change what he had done.

The Mountain of Fear and the Mountain of Joy

*18 You have not come to a mountain that can be touched, and that is burning with fire; to darkness, gloom and storm; 19 to a trumpet blast or to such a voice speaking words that those who heard it begged that no further word be spoken to them," **(Hebrews 12: 1 - 19 NIV)***

This encourages us to keep on fighting until we depart this world. Many blessings will be released here on earth in accordance with the person of God. A deliverer, a provider, a healer, a comforter, a shield and butler, a defender, a savior, a redeemer, a way maker, and the endless list of who He is - summarized as "I AM THAT I AM. The ultimate blessing, though, is to wear the crown of life and reign with Him forever. *Hebrews 12* warns us of faith fatigue and the urge to let down our guards. But, we have to continue fighting the fight of faith until the Lord calls us home.

OLAYINKA OLUSOLA AKISANYA